HISTORY OF FUN STUFF

True Colors!
The Story of Crayola

By Jesse Burton
Illustrated by Scott Burroughs

Ready-to-Read

Simon Spotlight
New York   London   Toronto   Sydney   New Delhi

SIMON SPOTLIGHT
An imprint of Simon & Schuster Children's Publishing Division
1230 Avenue of the Americas, New York, New York 10020
This Simon Spotlight edition October 2018
© 2018 Crayola, Easton, PA. 18044-0431. Crayola Oval Logo®, Crayola®, Chevron Design®, and
Serpentine Design® are registered trademarks of Crayola used under license.
All rights reserved, including the right of reproduction in whole or in part in any form.
SIMON SPOTLIGHT, READY-TO-READ, and colophon are registered trademarks of Simon & Schuster, Inc.
For information about special discounts for bulk purchases, please contact Simon & Schuster Special Sales at
1-866-506-1949 or business@simonandschuster.com.
Manufactured in the United States of America 0818 LAK
Library of Congress Cataloging-in-Publication Data
Names: Burton, Jesse, author. | Burroughs, Scott, illustrator. Title: True colors! : the story of Crayola /
by Jesse Burton ; illustrated by Scott Burroughs. Description: New York : Simon Spotlight, 2018. | Series:
Ready-to-Read | Series: History of fun stuff | Audience: Ages 6-8. | Audience: K to Grade 3.
Identifiers: LCCN 2018026477 (print) | LCCN 2018028961 (ebook) | ISBN 9781534425682 (e-book) |
ISBN 9781534425675 (hardback) | ISBN 9781534425668 (pbk) Subjects: LCSH: Crayola (Firm)—Juvenile
literature. | Crayons—History—Juvenile literature. | Artists' materials industry—United States—History—
Juvenile literature. | BISAC: JUVENILE NONFICTION / Readers / Beginner. | JUVENILE NONFICTION /
Art / Drawing. | JUVENILE NONFICTION / Media Tie-In. Classification: LCC HD9791.U54 (ebook) |
LCC HD9791.U54 C7338 2018 (print) | DDC 338.7/667—dc23
LC record available at https://lccn.loc.gov/2018026477

CONTENTS

Chapter 1: Coloring B.C.
  (Before Crayola)   4
Chapter 2: Cousins in Color   12
Chapter 3: An Explosion of Color   20
Chapter 4: Coloring in the Future   30
But Wait . . . There's More!   37

CHAPTER 1
Coloring B.C. (Before Crayola)

What inspires you to draw a picture? Is it a new experience like a family trip? Do you like to draw pictures of people you know? Or do you tap into your imagination and draw objects from dreams and even patterns and symbols? Whatever your inspiration, chances are you grabbed a box of crayons and paper to make some colorful art. But what did people do before crayons existed? How did their drawing tools look and feel?

Throughout history people have been drawn to drawing in color. There are examples of drawings as far back as 37,500 BCE, when people drew and painted objects and symbols from their everyday lives. For example, the Lascaux Caves of France (15,000 BCE) include more than six hundred paintings and drawings, showing all kinds of animals, like horses, deer, cows, and cats. There are symbols on the cave walls, too. Prehistory experts determined that these ancient painters used materials they could easily find, like red and yellow ocher. Ocher is made of minerals and clay found in the earth.

The ancient Greeks and Romans (650 BCE) also looked to the earth for drawing resources. They combined colored pigment from natural products like clay and berries with hot wax. Once cooled, they would begin to paint. When the painting was finished, they would cover the image with more hot wax, sealing it in place. It was messy and took a lot of time. This method is called encaustic painting. The word "encaustic" comes from the Greek language and it means "to burn in."

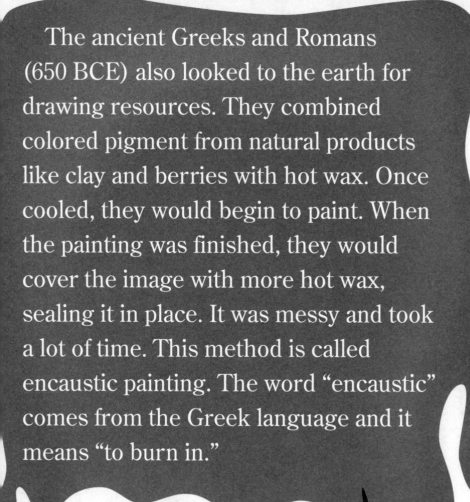

Ancient cultures also drew with charcoal. What could be easier than drawing with a charred stick? It was easy to apply and the supply was endless. Over time the process of making charcoal was refined. In the middle ages artists would bake a batch of charcoal sticks. First they tied together a few twigs with wire. Then they would put the bundle in a clay pot and lay the pot in the ash of a dying fire overnight. When they woke up they'd have a new set of charcoal sticks.

Some artists found ways to create masterpieces using charcoal only. But everyday people who simply wanted to draw found charcoal hard to use. It was easy to smudge. And there was only slight variation in the color it produced.

As time marched on, more and more drawing tools were created. Chalk sticks, pencils, and paint. They all had their drawbacks. It was hard to preserve an image drawn in chalk. At the time, pencils were only one color. And it took a lot of time and patience to create with paint. What could casual artists use to draw?

In the late 1700s, Nicolas-Jacques Conté, a French scientist, invented an art stick made of clay and graphite, the soft, black mineral used in pencils. The art stick would be cured with fire in a kiln, or oven. It was much easier to hold these art sticks, plus they didn't smudge! While it didn't cost a lot of money to make what are called Conté sticks, they were not very colorful. Nearly forty years later, another French inventor added wax to the formula. His name was Joseph Lemercier, and he is considered to be the creator of the wax-based crayon.

CHAPTER 2
Cousins in Color

Over the next few decades a number of companies developed different types of wax-based crayons. It was hard to keep up with the demand, especially in the United States of America. American schools were adding art classes to the curriculum, and children were going to school at a younger age. What tools could they use? Luckily, a creative team of businessmen found the answer to this question.

In 1885, Edwin Binney was put in charge of his family's company, a chemical factory in upstate New York. His partner was his cousin C. Harold Smith. They called their company Binney & Smith. The factory produced red iron-oxide pigments. These man-made powders from natural elements were mixed into red paint used on barns across America. They also produced a carbon black pigment that was used to strengthen car tires.

Edwin focused on creating new products, while C. Harold traveled across the country selling their creations. They bought a mill in Easton, Pennsylvania, and began making products at this new location. There they made slate pencils for students to use on their slate boards, and dustless chalk. Before this innovation, classrooms had been filled with clouds of chalk dust every time a teacher or students wrote on the blackboard.

This dustless chalk was such a huge improvement that Binney & Smith went to the 1904 World's Fair in Saint Louis and demonstrated their invention. Everyone wanted to use this remarkable chalk! They even won a gold medal at the fair.

At the same time dustless chalk was
making news, the cousins stayed focused
on the classroom. What was needed in the
classroom? Teachers needed stronger,

16

more colorful crayons that did not smell
and were not expensive. Binney & Smith
were up to the challenge.

In 1903, the company produced their first box of crayons. These crayons, made with paraffin wax, did not include any harmful ingredients, they didn't break, and they were very colorful. And they only cost five cents a  box! Children could color in the classroom and at home. Everyday artists only needed a nickel and their imagination.

Speaking of imagination . . . Binney & Smith kept creating new, exciting products like special sets of crayons and paint for fine artists. And they always returned to the classroom. Teachers had lots of ideas, and Binney and Smith listened.

One teacher in particular had something important to say on this subject. Binney's wife, Alice, had been a schoolteacher. As her husband and his cousin developed their revolutionary crayon, she suggested that they call the product "Crayola," which comes from *craie*, the French word for chalk, and *ola* for oleaginous (oh-LEE-agin-us), which is another word for oily.

CHAPTER 3
An Explosion of Color

With each decade, new generations of Crayola crayon fans were born. Binney & Smith remained focused on the coloring experience of children. In 1936, the company worked with other manufacturers of arts and crafts products to form an

organization that promoted the creation of safe art materials. As new arts and crafts products were developed, they had to meet safety standards in order to earn a certificate and seal. The seal appeared on the product and let consumers know that the material inside was safe to use.

Back at the Binney & Smith factory, new, exciting products were being developed. A bigger, brighter box of crayons was created. It contained sixty-four colors, and even had a built-in crayon sharpener. Boxes of crayons rolled off the assembly line.

Binney & Smith never stopped dreaming up new, inventive products for more and more people. In 1987 the company introduced washable markers. Five years later, washable crayons were created. Parents no longer needed to

worry about the littlest artists leaving their mark. The company would go on to develop a line of paint and paint supplies for professional artists. There was a product for every type of artist.

Thanks to Binney & Smith, coloring
became an extrasensory experience. In
1994, Magic Scents crayons were created.
Now children could color, and their

artwork was scented. For example, a pink
crayon smelled like bubble gum, while
a green crayon smelled like pine trees.
Imagine the color and scent combinations!

During this same time period, the company decided that crayons weren't just products. They could be part of a live event. So they opened the original Crayola Factory in Easton, Pennsylvania, to visitors, who learned about, played with, and created with crayons. This artistic

space included games, demonstrations, and hands-on activities. In recent years the name was changed to Crayola Experience. Three more sites have opened—in Florida, Minnesota, and Texas. And in 2007, Binney & Smith changed its name to Crayola!

CHAPTER 4
Coloring in the Future

Today you can find Crayola crayons just about anywhere in the world. They are so popular that even the naming of a new crayon or the retirement of another color makes the news. In 2017, Crayola introduced a new crayon, called bluetiful.™ The color was inspired by a newly discovered pigment. Scientists formed this pigment when they mixed a dark black oxide with chemicals, and heated the combination, which turned bright blue. People are very excited about their favorite colors, so Crayola often asks the public to vote for their favorite color in a Color Census. When people voted in the year 2000, the top picks included: midnight blue, aquamarine, periwinkle, denim, cerulean, and blizzard blue.

Crayola is also leading the way with creative ways to be kind to the environment. The Crayola Solar Farm is made up of thirty thousand solar panels. These panels are built to absorb the sun's light and convert it into energy. The solar panels at the Crayola Solar Farm make enough power to produce one billion Crayola crayons and five hundred million markers a year!

Solar energy is power obtained from sunlight. When sunlight hits the panels, cells inside each panel convert the light energy into electrical currents. The electrical currents supply the power for Crayola's factory.

The Crayola ColorCycle program is another way the company helps the environment. In this program, Crayola works with children from kindergarten through twelfth grade to collect used-up markers from the classroom. Crayola sends them to companies that use the most advanced conversion technologies available today to make fuel blends, wax compounds for asphalt and roofing shingles, and to

generate electricity—so most of that plastic doesn't go into landfills. Crayola is also on the lookout for new technologies as they become available. Just like those two colorful cousins—Binney and Smith—the people who work at Crayola today come up with products and solutions so children and adults have more ways than ever to be creative.

HISTORY
OF FUN STUFF
EXPERT
ON
CRAYOLA
CRAYONS

Congratulations! You've reached the end of this book and are now an official History of Fun Stuff Expert on Crayola crayons. So the next time you open a new box of crayons, remember all you know about how these little, colorful sticks became an American institution!

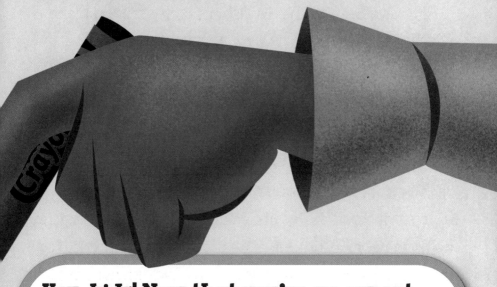

Hey, kids! Now that you're an expert on the history of crayons, turn the page to learn even more about crayons, and some more historical facts along the way!

Meet Me at the Fair

World's fairs are known for introducing new technology and inventions. And the 1904 World's Fair in St. Louis, Missouri, was no exception. Crayola was one of many companies with exciting products on display there. World's fairs continue to be held today. One is planned for 2020 in Dubai. Here are two innovations that debuted at the 1904 fair:

X-ray Machine

If you've been to the dentist or taken a trip by plane, then you've likely had an X-ray picture taken. These machines send powerful waves of energy through objects that light cannot pass through. They take pictures inside the object, like teeth or a suitcase at the airport.

Waffle Cone

Ice cream was a popular treat at the fair, which ran from April through December, most especially during the hot summer months. One day an ice cream vendor sold so many scoops that he ran out of cups! Luckily his stand was next to Ernest A. Hamwi's, a man from Syria who was selling *zalabia*—a thin, crispy pastry that looked like a flat waffle. Mr. Hamwi had an idea! He rolled his pastry into a cone while it was still hot. Once the cone cooled off, the ice cream vendor put a few scoops in it. And the rest is history.

Find Your Inner Abstract Artist

Important: Ask an adult for assistance with this project.

Would you like to make some abstract art? Here's what you'll need for this project:

- 3 large crayons
- tape
- drawing paper
- hair dryer

Tie or tape three large crayons together.

Tape a piece of drawing paper to a table.

As you hold the crayons, ask the adult to turn the hair dryer on a low heat setting. They should blow heat directly onto the crayons until they begin to melt.

Move your hand around over the paper to create abstract images. Try different color combinations and layer colors over colors.

Let the melted crayon drippings dry for at least thirty minutes before removing the tape and drawing paper from the table.

Being an expert on something means you can get an awesome score on a quiz on that subject! Take this

HISTORY OF CRAYOLA QUIZ

to see how much you've learned.

1. "Encaustic" comes from the Greek language and it means to:
   a. color inside the lines   b. burn in   c. erase

2. During the middle ages, people baked charcoal sticks in a:
   a. clay pot   b. microwave   c. kettle of boiling water

3. Binney & Smith won a gold medal at the 1904 World's Fair for their invention of:
   a. an X-ray machine   b. ice cream   c. dustless chalk

4. The company produced the first box of Crayola crayons in:
   a. 1903   b. 1930   c. 1979

5. The first box of Crayola crayons cost:
   a. fifty cents   b. five cents   c. five dollars

6. The original scented crayons included scents like:
   a. bubble gum   b. mustard   c. rose and maple syrup
      and pine trees   and ketchup

7. Solar energy is power obtained from:
   a. rivers   b. sunlight   c. wind

8. In 2017, Crayola introduced a new color. Its name is:
   a. periwinkle   b. bluetiful   c. denim

Answers: 1. b 2. a 3. c 4. a 5. b 6. a 7. b 8. b